Editor
Janet Cain, M.Ed.

Managing Editor
Ina Massler Levin, M.A.

Editor-in-Chief
Sharon Coan, M.S. Ed.

Illustrator
Ken Tunell

Cover Artist
Barb Lorseyedi

Art Coordinator
Kevin Barnes

Art Director
CJae Froshay

Imaging
Alfred Lau
Temo Parra
James Edward Grace

Product Manager
Phil Garcia

Publisher
Mary D. Smith, M.S. Ed.

Practice Makes Perfect

Cursive Writing

Teacher Created Resources

Author

Teacher Created Resources Staff

Teacher Created Resources, Inc.
6421 Industy Way
Westminster, CA 92683
www.teachercreated.com

ISBN: 978-0-7439-3331-5

©2002 Teacher Created Resources, Inc.
Reprinted, 2014

Made in the U.S.A.

Table of Contents

Introduction

The old adage "practice makes perfect" can really hold true for your child and his or her education. The more practice and exposure your child has with concepts being taught in school, the more success he or she is likely to find. For many parents, knowing how to help their children may be frustrating because the resources may not be readily available.

As a parent, it is also difficult to know where to focus your efforts so that the extra practice your child receives at home supports what he or she is learning in school.

This book has been written to help parents and teachers reinforce basic skills with children. *Practice Makes Perfect: Cursive Handwriting* helps children learn to correctly form the uppercase and lowercase forms of each letter. The exercises in this book can be done sequentially or can be taken out of order, as needed.

The following standards or objectives will be met or reinforced by completing the practice pages included in this book. These standards and objectives are similar to the ones required by your state and school district.

- The student will demonstrate competence in writing the cursive forms of each uppercase and lowercase letter.

- The student will increase control of pencil grip, paper position, stroke, and posture.

- The student will demonstrate competence in writing words legibly in cursive handwriting, using correct letter formation, appropriate size, and spacing.

How to Make the Most of This Book

Here are some useful ideas for making the most of this book:

- Set aside a specific place in your home to work on this book. Keep it neat and tidy, with the necessary materials on hand.

- Set up a certain time of day to work on these practice pages to establish consistency, or look for times in your day or week that are less hectic and more conducive to practicing skills.

- Keep all practice sessions with your child positive and constructive. If your child becomes frustrated or tense, set the book aside and look for another time to practice. Forcing your child to perform will not help. Do not use this book as a punishment.

- Help beginning readers with instructions.

- Review the work your child has done.

- Pay attention to the areas in which your child has the most difficulty. Provide extra guidance and exercises in those areas.

- Look for ways to make real-life application to the skills being reinforced. Play games such as having your child write lists with you.

The Alphabet

Aa Bb Cc Dd

Ee Ff Gg Hh

Ii Jj Kk Ll

Mm Nn Oo Pp

Qq Rr Ss Tt

Uu Vv Ww Xx

Yy Zz

Lines and Loops

Curves

C C C

c c c

c c c

∿∿∿

N N N

mmm

acrobatic

arachnid

a a a a a

a

a a a a a

a

busy
beaver

clever

cow

C C C C C

C

c c c c c

c

divine

dessert

$\mathcal{D}$ $\mathcal{D}$ $\mathcal{D}$ $\mathcal{D}$ $\mathcal{D}$

$\mathcal{D}$

d d d d d

d

elegant

elephant

E   E   E   E   E

E

l   l   l   l   l

l

fabulous
fudge

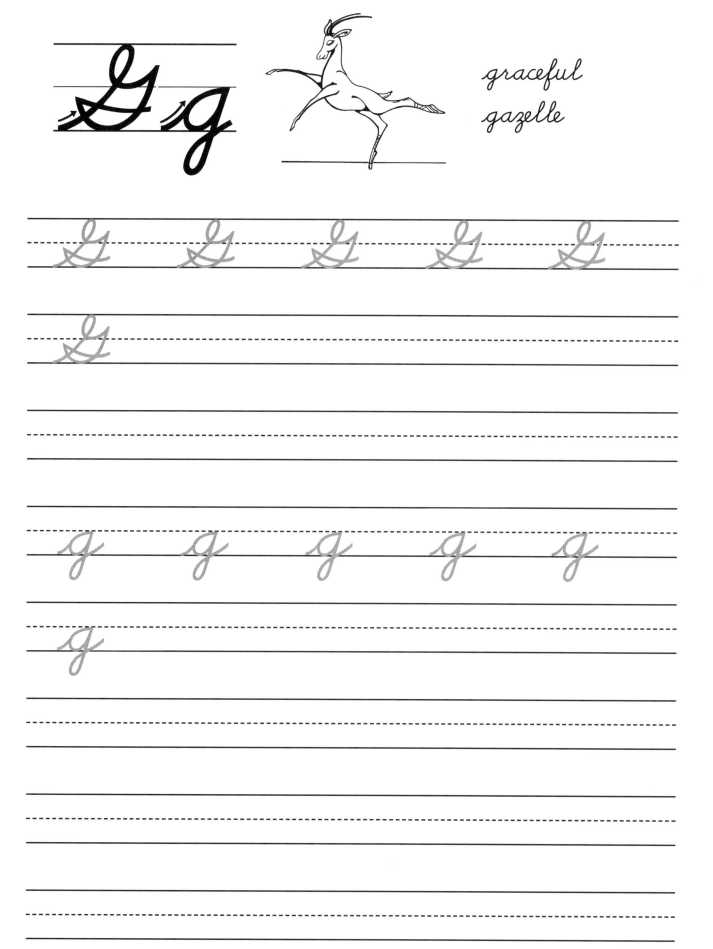

graceful
gazelle

happy

hippo

$\mathcal{H}$ $\mathcal{H}$ $\mathcal{H}$ $\mathcal{H}$ $\mathcal{H}$

$\mathcal{H}$

h h h h h

h

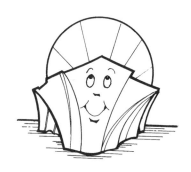

incredible
iceberg

l l l l l l

l

i i i i i

i

jumping

jackrabbit

kicking

kangaroo

K K K K K

K

k k k k k

k

luscious
lollipop

$\mathcal{L}$ $\mathcal{L}$ $\mathcal{L}$ $\mathcal{L}$ $\mathcal{L}$

$\mathcal{L}$

ℓ ℓ ℓ ℓ ℓ

ℓ

marvelous

milkshake

𝓝𝓃

nifty
necktie

𝓃 𝓃 𝓃 𝓃 𝓃

𝓃

𝓃 𝓃 𝓃 𝓃 𝓃

𝓃

odd

octopus

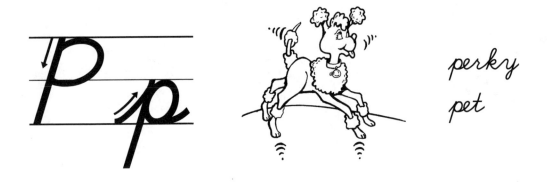

perky

pet

P P P P P

P

p p p p p

p

quick
quail

Q   Q   Q   Q   Q

Q

q   q   q   q   q

q

R r

refined

rat

R R R R R

R

r r r r r

r

sleek

seal

$\mathcal{S}$ $\mathcal{S}$ $\mathcal{S}$ $\mathcal{S}$ $\mathcal{S}$

$\mathcal{S}$

s s s s s

s

tasty

treat

$\mathcal{T}$ $\mathcal{T}$ $\mathcal{T}$ $\mathcal{T}$ $\mathcal{T}$

$\mathcal{T}$

t t t t t

t

$\mathcal{U}\,\mathcal{u}$

unique
umbrella

$\mathcal{U}$ $\mathcal{U}$ $\mathcal{U}$ $\mathcal{U}$ $\mathcal{U}$

$\mathcal{U}$

$\mathcal{u}$ $\mathcal{u}$ $\mathcal{u}$ $\mathcal{u}$ $\mathcal{u}$

$\mathcal{u}$

venomous
viper

wiggly

worm

$\mathcal{U}$ $\mathcal{U}$ $\mathcal{U}$ $\mathcal{U}$ $\mathcal{U}$

$\mathcal{U}$

w w w w w

w

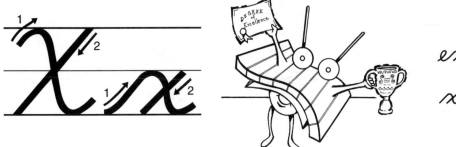

excellent
xylophone

𝒳 𝒳 𝒳 𝒳 𝒳

𝒳

𝓍 𝓍 𝓍 𝓍 𝓍

𝓍

yummy

yam

$\mathcal{Y}$ $\mathcal{Y}$ $\mathcal{Y}$ $\mathcal{Y}$ $\mathcal{Y}$

$\mathcal{Y}$

y y y y y

y

zealous

zebra

Ascenders

b

d

f

h

k

l

t

Descenders

g

j

p

q

y

z

g   j   p   q   y   z

Consonant Combinations

bl   bl

bloom

fl   fl

flame

gl   gl

glass

Consonant Combinations *(cont.)*

br   *br*

brush

cr   *cr*

crow

dr   *dr*

drain

Consonant Combinations *(cont.)*

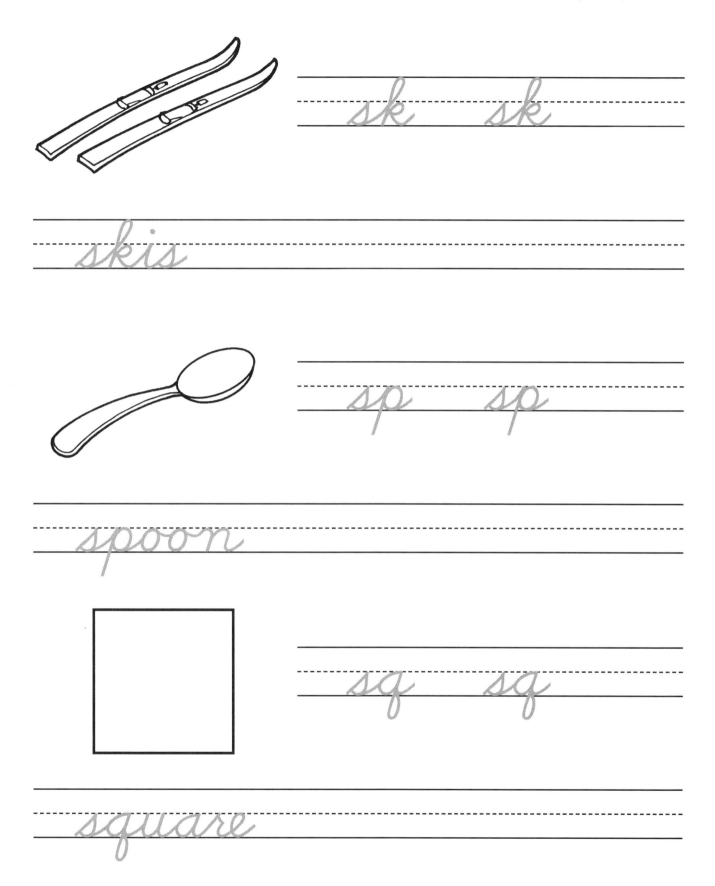

sk   *sk*

skis

sp   *sp*

spoon

sq   *sq*

square

Consonant Combinations *(cont.)*

ch   ch

chain

sh   sh

shoe

wh   wh

wheel

Consonant Combinations *(cont.)*

kn   *kn*

knit

mb   *mb*

comb

wr   *wr*

wreath

Consonant Combinations *(cont.)*

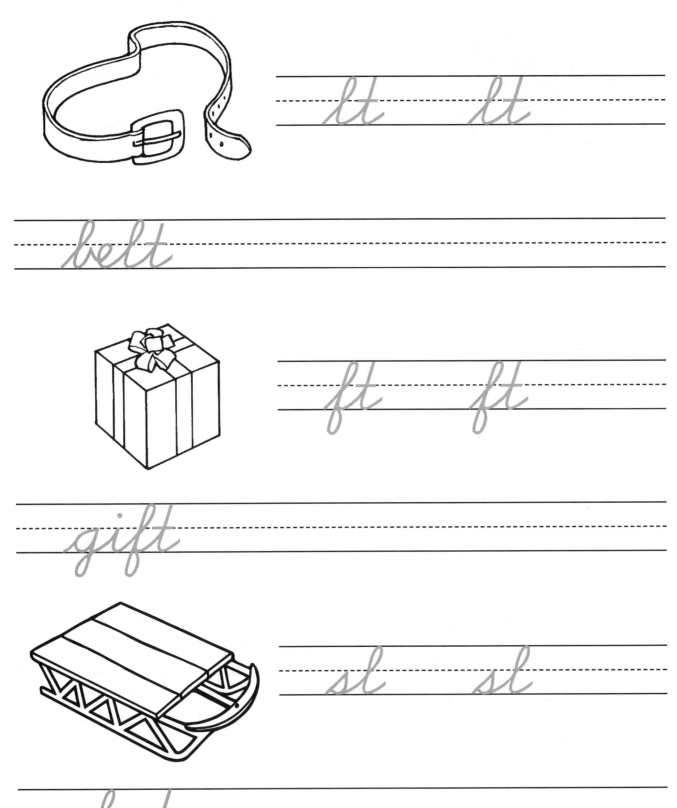

lt   lt

belt

ft   ft

gift

sl   sl

sled

Vowel Combinations

ai   *ai*

train

oa   *oa*

boat

ay   *ay*

pay

Vowel Combinations *(cont.)*

ea   ea

read

ee   ee

sleep

ie   ie

thief

42

Vowel Combinations (cont.)

oa   oa

foal

oo   oo

book

ou   ou

house

Months

January

February

March

Months *(cont.)*

April

May

June

Months (cont.)

July

August

September

Months *(cont.)*

October

November

December

Practice Page